WINES
OF THE WORLD

Bernard Moore

Published by Roydon Publishing Co. Ltd. 1984
London
England

ISBN 0946674 264

Printed in Portugal

Produced by Talos Books Limited
Lincolnshire, Great Britain

Edited by Diane Moore
Designed by Brian Benson
Picture Research by Jonathan Moore
Phototypesetting by Swiftprint Ltd, Stamford, Lincs.

WINES
OF THE WORLD

Bernard Moore

INTRODUCTION

What **is** all this business about wine? After all, it is only a drink. It comes in bottles like beer, cider, orangeade and lemonade. Like them it is made from natural fruit, is refreshing and, like beer and cider, thanks to alcoholic content, induces an agreeable condition of well-being - and even of self-admiration.

Yet everybody recognises that wine falls in a special category. It has its own language, a long and fascinating history, experts, some with an exaggerated and often precious way of talking, and, above all, a host of people, millions throughout the world, who drink it and like it, so go on drinking it. Not all of them, by any means, are experts or have fine taste. The great majority know what they like, but prices being what they are, usually have to be satisfied, except on special occasions, with something lower than their ambitions.

The comparison with beer and cider is, in fact, a facile one. Wine is made from the grape - the word comes from the Latin **vinea** for vineyard or vine - and your homemade elderberry, rhubarb and gooseberry "wines" are not really wines at all because they don't grow from the vine. And there are many varieties of grapes. Even those of the same family may develop different characteristics because of the climatic conditions to which they may be exposed, and the soil in which they are grown. The process of wine-making is described briefly later on, but it involves natural and human processes that not only make wine-making something of an art, but result in a wide range in quality.

Wine-making is age-old. The Egyptians were making it in 3000 B.C., but it was not new then. The Romans had their god of wine, Bacchus, and the Greeks theirs, Dionysus. It was, in fact, the Romans who laid down the pattern of the present-day world of wine. When their legions invaded Gaul and other parts of Europe they advanced along the river valleys, clearing stretches away from the banks. Here, in due course, they planted vines brought from their own country and the whole business began. By the time the Romans withdrew from Gaul after 500 years of occupation, wine-growing and wine-drinking were essential parts of French life and have continued to be.

As this book tells, there are today plenty of other countries with flourishing wine industries, and not only in Europe by any means. The United States is now one of the giants and there are significant industries in Australia and South Africa. But all the wine-producing countries have one thing in common. They fall in one of the two clearly defined geographical belts in which it is possible to produce wine. One is in the Northern Hemisphere roughly from 37°N to 48°, and the other in the Southern Hemisphere slightly closer to the Equator. In the northern belt, of course, we find the famous wine-growing countries of Europe - France, Germany, Italy, Spain, Portugal and the United States. In the

Far left: A leading wine producing area in Austria is the Weinviertel in Lower Austria between the Danube and the Czech frontier. It produces a light dry called Grüner Vertliner. Here grapes are being harvested at Mailberg. Left: Not all American wineries use modern equipment. Picture shows a hand-bottling machine at the Mon Ami Champagne Co, Ohio.

southern belt are principally Australia and South Africa but also parts of South America.

There is another thing that the wine-producing areas have in common - the general nature of the soil in which the grapes are grown. The vine likes gravelly soil providing good drainage, for it has a deep root system and digs down to absorb the minerals which are essential to the quality of the fruit. This is not to say that all vineyard soils are identical, indeed they are not. But it is no coincidence that many of the world's best vineyards are to be found on volcanic slopes or the rocky hills running down to rivers or lakes.

Broadly speaking, the vines, heavily pruned back in the preceding winter, sprout young shoots in the spring and it is then that they are particularly vulnerable to late frosts which can destroy the expected crop. By mid-summer, all being well, the small grapes are visible, grow and ripen in the summer months and are ready for picking in September or October. Heat and sunshine are needed to ensure the right sugar content in the grapes as it is the sugar that produces the alcohol during fermentation.

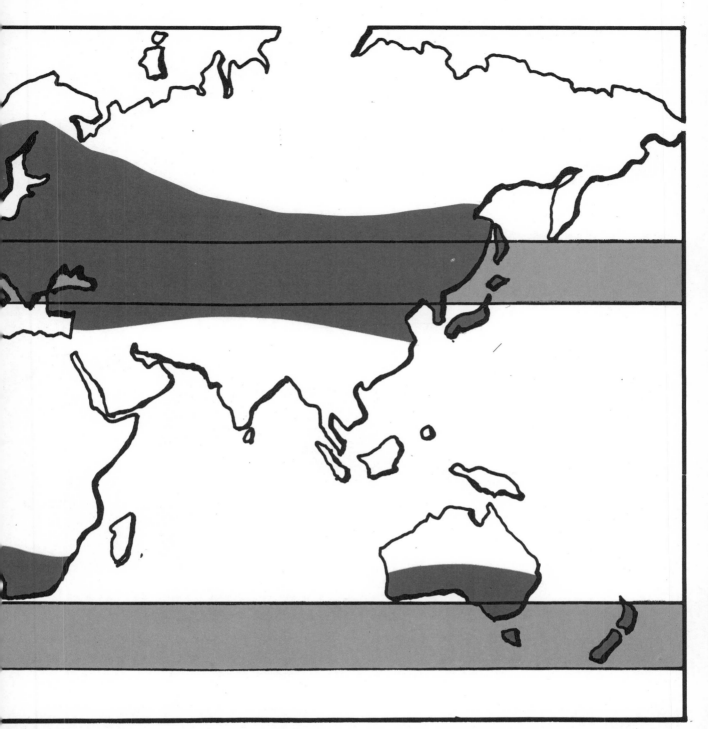

The grapes when picked and the stems removed are crushed without breaking the seeds and the juice allowed to ferment. This is brought about by the actions of natural yeasts already on the grape skins but these are often reinforced by other yeasts being added. The fermenting juice is called must. To make white wine the grape skins are removed from the must and if it is to be a sweet wine the fermentation is stopped while some of the natural sugar still remains. Fizzy white wines are bottled before fermentation is completed. To make red wines, the skins of the purple grapes are left in the must to

A map showing the main wine countries in the world. In the northern belt lie France, Germany, Italy, Spain, Portugal and the United States: in or near the southern, Australia, Argentina, Chile.

allow their colour to be absorbed: for rosé or pink wines the skins are left in the must for a shorter time. The process of fermentation takes about ten days or longer - the quicker the yeast works the better the fermentation - and the temperature is important with the must for white wine kept below 18°C, and that for red half as hot again.

9

Other processes follow; fining, clarification and ageing in oak barrels or glass or stainless steel containers and eventually bottling. As can be seen, so many processes involving human skill are involved that it is not surprising that wines appear in wide varieties, with different strength of alcohol, different lasting qualities, and above all different flavours. The basic principles of wine-making are the same throughout the world, it is the raw materials whose qualities result from soil and climatic conditions that introduce the first variations and the human element and the skill of the winemaker multiplies these.

In the chapters that follow, the main wine-producing areas of the world are described, as are the leading wines they produce. It should not be forgotten that while many countries have their own native grapes, these do not necessarily make good wines, and the picture that soon emerges is that most of the wines produced outside Europe, certainly their best, are now made from grapes originally of European stock. The wines of Argentina and Chile, for example, are largely made from Malbec, Cabernet Sauvignon and Pinot Noir grapes, and those of South Africa include those and others such as Chenin Blanc, Semillon and Riesling. In the United States, where a wine revolution is under way, the native American grape, noteworthy for its "foxy" flavour is being almost entirely replaced by vines of European stock.

This book is designed to give a global rather than a detailed picture of the world's wines. It will show that not only do national drinking tastes differ, but that they are constantly changing. A taste for dry wines, a sign of European sophistication, is rapidly taking over in North America where, in the past, sweetness and high alcoholic content were the popular taste. And a feature of the world wine scene in recent years has been the controls imposed by government to ensure that the buyer knows what he is buying. France, for example, has its system of "appellations contrôlées" which guarantees not only the origin of a wine but that it is of a certain standard; Italy and Germany have not dissimilar systems; and some of the states of the United States have quite rigorous rules. In Oregon, for example, wines are labelled showing the grapes from which they are made and they must be made from 90% of the named grapes.

Many hands make light work even though some of them may be small. This little Austrian girl is a willing assistant in working an ancient wine press in the province of Styria, whose capital is Graz. It is one of the smallest wine growing areas in Austria (which in the days of the old Austro-Hungarian Empire was a leading wine producing country) and lies only 50 miles north of Lutomer in Yugoslavia formerly part of the old empire.

11

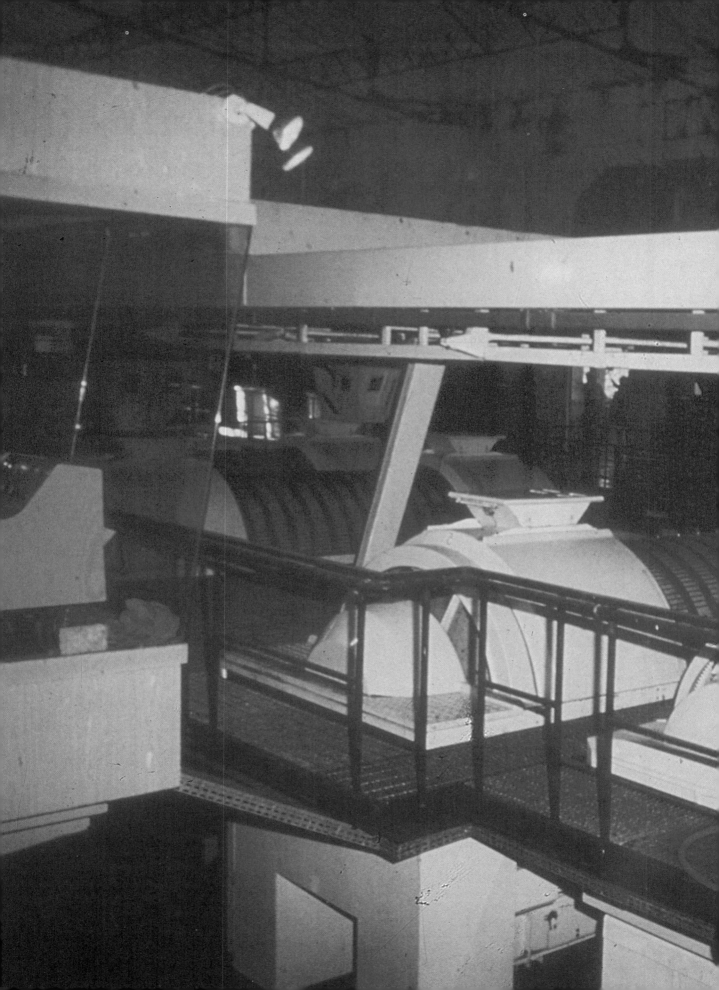

Left: Louis Pasteur, the famous French chemist, became an authority on wine when in the 1860s he was told by Emperor Napoleon III to investigate why so much wine deteriorated. He studied all aspects of wine making and wine storing, the effects of oxygen on fermentation etc. and, of course, pressures. Here is a modern pressurisation system in a French winery. *Below:* Modern harvesting in Canada. Canada has a flourishing and growing wine industry. One of its oldest wineries is Brights at Niagara Falls where for over 100 years many wines have been produced including their President Champagne made by the méthode Champenoise which won the grand gold medal at Ljubljana in 1979. The winery produces scores of wines - whites, reds, sherries and ports and a sparkling pink Spumanti with the endearing name of Pussycat. *Bottom:* In contrast to the modern harvester above here is one of the traditional brick-vaulted cellars where Châteauneuf-du-Pape, the famous Côte du Rhône wine of France is maturing. Châteauneuf dates back to the first Avignon Pope, Clément V who moved the papal court from Rome to Avignon in the fourteenth century. There he built his new chateau and established its vineyards.

Left: *"Fining" new wine at Freemark Abbey in St. Helena, California. "Fining" consists of pouring into the barrels beaten egg-whites which causes suspended solids to be carried to the bottom. The clear wine can then be "racked", that is to say drawn off from above the lees. Isinglass or even oxblood is sometimes used instead of egg-white. Freemark Abbey Winery is in the famous Napa Valley of California and produces mostly white wines of good repute. It was built in 1886 by a woman and later had the distinction of being owned by a man with the felicitous name of Swig. At the beginning of this century the then Italian owner discovered an untapped market for his red wine which he shipped to the other side of the U.S.A. to the granite and marble quarries of Vermont where there were many Italian immigrant workers.*

Below: *Aging barrels at the Paul Masson Champagne and Aging Cellars in Saratoga in California. A sample is being drawn off. Paul Masson wines are probably among the best known of the American wines in Europe, and indeed Paul Masson Vineyards are the largest exporters of wines from the United States. The story of the Paul Masson Vineyards began in 1852, when a **vigneron** from Bordeaux named Etienne Thee came to California and pioneered wine-growing in the Santa Clara Valley. He was succeeded by his son-in-law, Charles Lefranc, who in turn was succeeded by his son-in-law, Paul Masson. Paul Masson Vineyards have expanded greatly since 1936 and in 1961, they began planting the Pinnacles Vineyards in Monterey County.*

15

The château and vineyards where one of France's most famous burgundies, Château Clos Vougeot is produced. The château was once a monastery.

THE WINES OF FRANCE

The French have a jolly little drinking song which modestly sums up their attitude:

"Boire un petit coup c'est agréeable,

Boire un petit coup c'est doux", which means: "To drink a little glass is both agreeable and pleasant." To give them credit, the song goes on to warn against rolling under the table.

To the majority of French people wine is not, as it is in so many countries, an occasional celebratory luxury, but a commonplace fact of life, a normal accompaniment to a meal, or just by itself. French men and women may produce as much as 65,000,000 hectolitres of wine of one sort or another each year, and they show their faith in their own product by drinking about 54,000,000 of it themselves. In most countries people choose their wine to go with the food they are eating. In France it is by no means unknown to find dishes selected to go with wines already chosen.

In no other country in the world would an officer halt his troops in order for them to present arms to a vineyard, but that is just what a famous French leader made his soldiers do in the days of Napoleon when they passed the vineyard of Clos Vougeot, where his favourite wine was produced. Another distinguished French soldier, the Marshal de Richelieu summed up the situation with inescapable French logic when he said of the famous **Château Haut-Brion**: "If God forbade drinking would he have made so good a wine?"

Even non-wine drinkers who could not name any foreign wine except perhaps Port and Sherry could readily name a few French wines - Champagne certainly, and Burgundy and Bordeaux (or Claret), and perhaps even the wines of the Rhône and the Loire. Partly this is due to France's long wine history, but much is owed to the quality of the wines that have been perpetuated. Incidentally, the word "Claret" in place of "Bordeaux" owes its perpetuation to the long wine association between France and Britain, for it was because of its clarity, or purity, of colour that the British, Bordeaux's main customer for centuries, gave it the name.

Some useful French wine terms:

Appellation d'Origine Contrôlée: *Government system which guarantees the origin of a particular wine and controls its standard (ADOC on labels).*

Brut: *Dry, in Champagne.*

Chambrer: *Bringing wine to room temperature.*

Cru Classé: *There are five leading classes of wine grown in the Médoc. Cru Classé may mean any one of them.*

Grand Cru: *The best of a particular grape harvest and its wine.*

Grand Vin (Alsace): *Containing over 11% alcohol.*

Pétillant: *Effervescent or sparkling.*

Premier Cru: *See Grand Cru.*

Remuage: *The regular twisting of Champagne bottles to dislodge sediment.*

Supérieur: *Contains 1% more alcohol than permitted minimum (Bordeaux).*

Tête de Cuvée: *See also Grand Cru.*

Vendange Tardive (Alsace): *Strong and sweet because of late picked grapes.*

V.D.Q.S Vins Délimités de Qualité Supérieure: *Part of the control system applying to wines not controlled by the law on required brands (App. d'O. Cont.).*

Vins de Pays: *Local wines with a minimum alcoholic content of 9.5% (part of the control system).*

There are many different grapes used sometimes in combination to produce wines with individual flavour. Here are the principal French varieties:

Cabernet Sauvignon: *Small, blue-green, thick-skinned. Makes some of the best wines of Bordeaux.*

Carignan: *A moderate quality purple grape producing much modest wine in the Midi.*

Chardonnay: *Pale green, basis of some of the best wines of Burgundy, and, with Pinot Noir, of Champagne.*

Chenin Blanc: *Gold and white coloured grape which makes the wines of Anjou and Touraine.*

Gamay: *The purple grape from which Beaujolais is made.*

Grenache: *Famous sweet purple grape used in the Rhône Valley wines such as Châteauneuf-du-Pape.*

Merlot: *An outstanding purple grape; the basis of the wines of St. Emilion & Pomerol.*

Pinot Noir: *Outstanding of all the wine grapes. Although red it is used in Champagne, but is better known as the basis of the famous wines of Burgundy - eg. Chambertin and Musigny.*

Sémillon: *A brownish-white grape, liable to "noble rot", and so producing an unusually sweet must used for fine sweet wines such as Sauternes.*

Syrah or Petit Sirah: *A red grape from the Rhône Valley, whose wines have lasting qualities.*

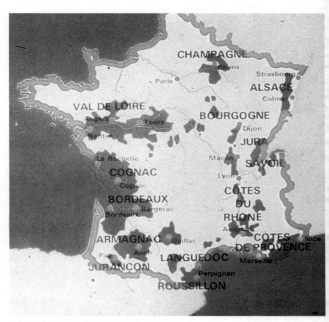

Map showing the main wine producing areas of France.

The popular idea of the French countryside is that it is a land covered by vineyards, and little else but this is far from the truth. The area of France is about 211,000 square miles, and that of its vineyards only about 5,000 square miles; a fairly small proportion. The famous wine-growing areas are: Burgundy, Bordeaux, Champagne, the Loire Valley, the Côtes du Rhône, and Alsace. There are other scattered areas - for instance the Jura, the Mediterranean coast and others, but those are the big six. What do they produce in the range of great wines, and those within the ordinary drinker's reach?

Burgundy: This is the least compact of the six, with Chablis, some 100 miles South-East of Paris forming a separate enclave, and as the most northerly, the most liable to frost damage. Chablis produces what is perhaps the world's most famous still white wine, one copied throughout the wine world. Made from the Chardonnay grape, it is pale gold in colour, slightly scented, and fresh to the taste; a worthy accompaniment to grilled fish, and shellfish especially.

Next down the Burgundy chain, about 100 miles south of Chablis, are the Côtes de Nuits, the Côtes de Beaune (sometimes coupled together as the Côte d'Or) which lie along the same hilly ridge from Dijon to the south-west. Here we start with the red wines which have made Burgundy famous. It seems incredible that so small an area could produce such famous wines as: Chambertin; Chambolle-Musigny; Clos Vougeot; Vosne-Romanée; Nuit St. Georges; Beaune; Aloxe-Corton; Montrachet; Meursault; Pommard; Volnay, and many others. The wines of the Côtes de Nuits are nearly all red, on the heavy side, and with a full bouquet, and go well with game and roasts, or grilled meat and cheese. The Côtes de Beaune, as will be seen from the above list, also produces outstanding white wines (eg. Montrachet, Meursault and Corton-Charlemagne) which are dry and mellow with a faint nutty flavour.

Next down in the Burgundy chain comes Mâcon, the area which takes its name from the town of the same name. It produces a number of ordinary red and white wines, but in one small area it produces, from Chardonnay grapes, the distinguished white Pouilly-Fuissé, dry and fragrant and its associates Pouilly-Loché and Pouilly-Vinzelles. A note of warning. Another distinguished white wine - Pouilly-Fumé - does not come from Mâcon but from the Loire Valley and is made from Sauvignon not Chardonnay grapes.

Finally in the Burgundy chain we come to one of the best known of all - Beaujolais. The wines from this area are by no means the finest of the Burgundies but they are soft and fruity, of good colour, and can be drunk while they are still young (a factor in keeping the prices down). The name Beaujolais has become so well-known generally that some of its best wines are overlooked. There are, for

example, Moulin à Vent, Morgon, Fleurie, Brouilly, Chenas, Julienas, all vintages with their own characteristics. All the Beaujolais are made from the Gamay grape, but nowhere is this so successful as in Beaujolais. This may be due to the granity nature of the soil of the area.

Côtes du Rhône: As its name indicates, this area lies along the banks of part of the River Rhône, south of Beaujolais, in a strip some 130 miles long between Vienne in the north and Avignon in the south. There is a marked difference between the wines produced in the north (including Hermitage) and those in the south (including the well-known Châteauneuf-du-Pape), and most wines of the area are made from a mixture of grapes rather than a single variety.

One of the best of the red Rhône wines, Côte Rôtie, comes from the very north of the strip, near Vienne, and an equally distinguished white from nearby Coudrieu. But perhaps best-known of the northern wines are those from Hermitage, both reds and whites, the former rather heady and fragrant, the latter dry and aromatic.

Best known in the southern part of the Côtes du Rhône area is, of course, Châteauneuf-du-Pape, with a 12.5% alcoholic content. It has a historical connection with a well-known Bordeaux wine Château Papa Clément. Papa Clément was a gentleman named Bertrand de Got who was Cardinal Archbishop of Bordeaux in the 14th century, and became the first French Pope as Clément V. In 1309 he moved the papal court from Rome to Avignon, thus becoming the first of the Avignon popes. His new house, or châteauneuf, was planted up with the now famous vineyards so that one can choose between a papal claret or a papal burgundy as it were.

The vine flourishes in volcanic or gravelly soil because of the help it gives to the deep-rooting system. Though the soil might not look promising, this vineyard produces one of France's best-known Côtes du Rhône wines, Châteauneuf du Pape.

The home of one of the finest wines of Bordeaux, Château Ansone, at St. Emilion. A number of communes are entitled under the appellations-Contrôlées rules to call their wines St. Emilion but it is the vineyards immediately around the town that produce grandes crus classé. Château Ansone produces a Premier Grande Cru Classé.

Bordeaux: It is not the least bit surprising that the wines of the Bordeaux region have been immensely popular throughout the centuries in England, for in the 12th century Henry II of England married Eleanor of Aquitaine, and for over 300 years, English princes and kings were Dukes of Aquitaine. English merchants settled in and around Bordeaux, and a flourishing export trade began, particularly to England. Each year an English wine fleet arrived off Bordeaux early in October, returning before Christmas with its cargoes of that year's wine, which was drunk young, as is Beaujolais today.

Today Bordeaux rivals Burgundy with fine wines, both red and white, and a host of more modest vintages. Its vineyards are more concentrated in a compact area bordering on the Bay of Biscay with the city of Bordeaux as its centre and divided into many areas: Médoc, Pauillac, Graves, St. Emilion, Pomerol, and Sauternes-Barsac. Their wines range from delicate light to full-bodied reds, and from fresh, dry to very sweet whites. From the Médoc, 50 miles long and less than 10 miles wide running beside the gravelly banks of the River Gironde come the wines of St. Estèphe, Château Lafite, Château Clos d'Estournel, Château Montrose, Château Phélan-Ségur noteworthy among them. Then, more southerly, the wines of Pauillac and St. Julien, with such famous names as Château Latour, Pontet Canet, Château Lynch-Bages, Mouton Rothschild, Château Talbot, Château Gruaud-La Rose and Château Leoville-Barton.

Next to the south comes Margaux, a town with, for its size, seemingly more wine-growing "châteaux" than proper or believable. The wines of Margaux from good years will age splendidly, full-flavoured and with a heavenly bouquet.

From the concentrated vineyards of the Médoc, we move further south to Graves, Sauternes and Barsac, known chiefly from their white wines, although some good red Graves are produced on the outskirts of the city of Bordeaux, notably Château Haut Brion (which Samuel Pepys drank over 300 years ago, calling it Ho Brion). Nearby is Château Papa Clément, mentioned already in connection with Châteauneuf-du-Pape. Sauternes and Barsac are famous for their sweet white wines, most famous of all Château Yquem, which alone has the title of First Great Growth. The area has the good fortune to suffer from "noble rot", a disease which leads to over-ripeness of the grape with an excess of sugar, hence the sweetness of the wines.

Last but not least by any means we come to the adjoining Pomerol and St. Emilion areas of Bordeaux. Under the French Appellation Contrôlée system only seven communes are entitled to call their wine St. Emilion, the picturesque town of that name, of course, and Lussac St. Emilion, Montagne St. Emilion, Parsac St. Emilion, Puisseguin St. Emilion, Sables St. Emilion and St. Georges St.

Emilion. All produce fine, full-blooded red wine, as do the vineyards of Pomerol, notably those of Fronsac on the River Gironde, and Blaye on the Dordogne. The latter also produces white wines.

Champagne: The French zealously guard the name Champagne, refusing to recognise any so-called wine that does not come from the clearly-defined Champagne country, with its centre at Rheims, some 75 miles east of Paris. To drive through the Champagne country, with its closely-packed vineyards, most of them clearly labelled, is like taking a ride through a wine-list. Names such as Heidsieck, Veuve-Clicquot, Mumm, Roederer, Taittinger, Moët & Chandon, Pol Roger, Perrier & Jouet, and a dozen others flash by.

Although it is a white wine, Champagne is usually made from a combination of Chardonnay and Pinot Noir grapes, the latter having to be carefully handled to avoid colouration of the wine. Making Champagne is a complicated business. It begins as a normal still white wine, the must of the cuvée being allowed to ferment and stand for two months or more, when its sugar content will have become alcohol. It is then blended, a process which brings out the skill of the winemaker, and a further fermentation period follows. Bottling takes place about six months after the grape harvest and at this time a sugared Champagne with a yeast starter (liqueur de tirage) is added, causing further fermentation and creating carbonic acid gas. The sealed bottles are then stacked in chalk tunnels where fermentation continues slowly, the bottles being regularly turned to prevent sediment forming. This is called remuage. Finally the bottle is permanently sealed with a cork designed to resist gas pressure. As this is done, all sediment is removed and a small mixture of sugar champagne and brandy added before the cork is wired on.

Champagne has a language of its own:

Blanc de blancs: *White grapes only are used.*
Brut: *Very dry.*
Demi Sec: *Very sweet.*
Extra Sec: *Dry.*
Jereboam: *Bottle containing equivalent of 4 bottles.*
Magnum: *Bottle containing equivalent of 2 bottles.*
Methuselah: *Bottle containing equivalent of 8 bottles.*
Nebuchadnezzar: *Bottle containing equivalent of 22 bottles.*

Many a celebration is ready made here in one of the chalk tunnels of the Champagne area where the wine of that name is stored and where fermentation continues slowly after bottling. Some of the wine, as can be seen is stored not flat but tilted, part of the complicated process known as "remuage" which is designed to prevent the formation of sediment. "Champagne" is produced in many parts of the world from California to Australia but the French adamantly refuse to recognise any wine under that name which is not produced in the Champagne area of France.

A vineyard of Muscadet in the light of a rainbow. Muscadet is the name of a grape and wine not of a place. The grape originated in Burgundy under another name but became Muscadet when it was introduced into Brittany and the Loire Valley, with which area especially that near the Alantic coast, it is now closely associated. **Inset:** Making wine storage barrels. In many places such as California and Australia barrels have been replaced by stainless steel and glass tanks. But many modern wine producers believe that oak barrels are still best for maturing red wines and (including California) import barrels from France for the purpose.

Rehoboam: *Bottle containing equivalent of 6 bottles.*
Rosé: *Champagne made pink by adding a little red wine.*
Sec: *Slightly sweet.*

Labels may be marked "vintage" or "non-vintage". "Vintage" is used only for a good year, the date being given on the label. Vintage Champagne must be matured in the bottle for at least three years. Non-Vintage Champagne is a blend of different years matured for at least one year.

It should not be forgotten that all the wines that come from Champagne are not "bubbly". There are extremely palatable still wines, red and white, which are not subjected to the "méthode champenoise" which produces the champagne that first comes to mind.

The Loire Valley: There can be little argument that the Loire rising in the Cevennes and flowing some 625 miles to Nantes in the Bay of Biscay, is the most beautiful of the French Rivers. It is famous for its Châteaux, and it also contains over 500,000 acres of vineyards, but, curiously, Château wines are comparatively rare, most of the wines being labelled according to district, village or vineyard. Most of the wines are white, the best known being the Muscadet produced from vineyards neighbouring on Nantes; Sancerre and Pouilly-Fumé (from Sauvignon grapes) some 60 miles south-east of Orléans: Vouvray near Tours, and Saumur, half way between Nantes and Tours.

Touraine, of which Tours is the capital, produces many wines, both red and white, pleasant, but (except from Vouvray) not particularly outstanding. The better white wines are made from Chenin Blanc, a white grape from nearby Anjou, and are excellent as dessert wines, if over-sweet for some tastes. Chinon and Bourgueil, further east, produce a sound sweet red wine made from Cabernet Franc grapes.

Alsace: It is hardly surprising that Alsace, neighbouring Germany, and, indeed, under German rule for nearly 50 years, should produce wines nearer to German than French types. Indeed, during their occupation from 1870 to 1918, the Germans deliberately sought to denigrate any reputation that Alsatian wine had previously enjoyed, which was not high in any case.

Today the situation is much improved. Although the vineyards of Alsace, mostly in the valleys of the eastern slopes of the Vosges, with the Rhine flowing further to the east, still grow little-known grapes and the wine therefrom used for local consumption; many have now been planted with finer varieties, such as Sylvaner, Muscat, Riesling, Pinot Gris and, particularly Traminer or Gewurtztraminer. Grand Cru is the Alsatian designation for the best wines from the best vineyards, and only Muscat, Pinot Gris, Riesling or Gewurtztraminer grapes may be used to make them. Two more common wines made

with blended grapes are Zwicker and Edelzwicker.

The foregoing are what might be described as the six principal wine-growing areas of France, but there are many more. For example the Jura and Savoie on the border of Switzerland producing, among others, Crépy, Seyssel and Arbois: the area of the Midi, huge, but with only two Appellation Contrôlée red wines, Fitou and Collivure, and a wide variety of white, particularly dessert wines: Provence etc..

The fact is that France, by no means the largest wine-producing country, is the most prolific in choice. Some of its wines are magnificent, many very good, many more just good, quite a lot indifferent, many poor.

Vive la France!

Above: What every vigneron hopes to see in the autumn - perfect bunches of grapes. Most grapes are still hand-picked, providing seasonal employment although many countries now use mechanical pickers. *Right:* A typical vineyard in Alsace. On the slopes of the Schoenberg Mountain in the Vosges it overlooks the roofs of the ancient picturesque town of Riquewih.

Looking down from a German vineyard to the noble sweep of the River Rhine. A typical view of the vineyard-covered slopes of the great river on whose banks are produced some of the country's greatest wines.

THE WINES OF GERMANY
& ITALY

Except for the fact that the two countries adjoin France, and with it form the elite of the wine countries, there is not much similarity between Germany and Italy as wine producers. This is not altogether surprising for a large part of German vineyards lie on the northern limits of the wine-growing belt, while those of Italy enjoy the balmy warmth of the Mediterranean summer. One result is that German wines, certainly the best, are mostly white, while Italian, one is tempted to say, are all colours of the rainbow. Although they both take their business of wine production seriously, there is an impression of haphazard variety on the Italian scene, while the German picture is more orderly.

Germany

Germany's vineyards are to be found in the south-west corner of the country mainly on the banks of the River Rhine and its tributaries the Moselle and the Nahe. As in France it was the Romans who first developed the growing of grapes for wine, and as early as the 9th and 10th centuries there was mention of vineyards at Rudesheim and Nierstein two of Germany's best-known, though not the best, wines today. And, also as in France, the church played a large part in developing and sustaining the growing of grapes and the making of wine. Charlemagne was particularly generous in donating land to the local archbishops and prelates, who developed much of it into vineyards. By the 12th and 13th centuries Rhenish wine was being exported - the King of England bought 22 tuns at the very reasonable price of 1½d per gallon in 1243. All German wines were known as Rhenish wines until the 17th century when the name Hock was given to them, and the term is in fairly general use even today. The name comes from Hockheim through which the Rhenish wine was shipped, and where good wines are still produced. Hockheim lies in the northern tip of the German wine region, and is slightly more northerly than the French Champagne area.

The German winegrowers are generous in the information they give on their labels, but the names can be somewhat bewildering.

Chief among them are:

Qualitatswein bestimmte Aubergebiete *is a quality wine from a specified region which has passed a tasting test.*

Qualitatswein mit Prädikat (Q.M.P.) *is high quality, unsugared wine.*

Auslese *a sweet wine made from very ripe grapes.*

Beerenauslese and **Trackenhausenauslese** *are made from even riper grapes, often those suffering from "noble rot".*

Kabinet, *the standard grade of Q.M.P., dryish.*
Spätlese, *sweeter than Kabinet, and with more body, but less sweet than Auslese. Made from ripe grapes.*
Sekt: *Quality sparkling wine.*
Eiswein: *Wine made from frozen grapes.*
Trocken Wein: *A very dry wine sometimes called* **Diabetiken Wein.**

The grapes chiefly used by German winemakers are first and foremost the yellowish-green Riesling, the basis for their quality wines. Others are the early-ripening Sylvaner, the pinkish Traminer (or Gewurztraminer), the Muller-Thurgau, a cross between Riesling and Sylvaner; and a new grape, Kerner, a cross between Riesling and red Trollinger.

As can be seen from the map, the River Rhine flows westward forming the northern frontier of Switzerland, turns sharply north at Basle, and flows more or less north for 80 or so miles to near Karlsruhe, forming the frontier with France. At Karlsruhe the frontier turns westwards while the Rhine continues to flow northwards via Bingen, where it is joined by the River Nahe, then to Koblenz where it is joined by the Moselle, and then northwards via Cologne to the North Sea. It is the area from Basle to Koblenz which embraces the wine-producing region, especially the pocket

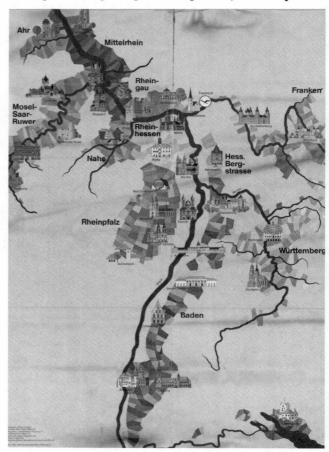

The Rhine River in Germany is famous for both the quality wines produced from grapes grown on its hill-sides, and for its many picturesque castles.

formed where the French frontier swings west near Karlsruhe, and then north, and which contains the Rivers Saar, Nahe and Moselle.

South of Karlsruhe in the Baden-Württemberg area between the Rhine and the Black Forest some wine is produced, but little of noteworthy quality. There is some produced in Ortenau south of Baden-Baden, but the vineyards of this southern region are scattered and mainly small. In the most southerly part, near Freiburg at Kaisersbuhl there is a large cooperative (wine cooperatives are frequent in the Upper Rhine area) which yields popular wines fuller and stronger than most wines grown in the region, and made from Rulander (Pinot Gris) grapes. Although, as has been said, the great majority of German wines are white, more reds than whites are produced in this Upper Rhine area including Oberotweilers, Kairchberg, Klosterberg, Brackenheim and Schwaigern.

A more important area to the north is Rheinhessen, famous for two things - the origination of the name Liebfraumilch, and the production of Niersteiner, two of the best-known German wines today. The story of Liebfraumilch is a strange one, and has nothing to do with milk. It began with the vineyard of a church in Worms - the Liebrfauenstift, and, say the experts, the wine was originally Liebfrauminch, minch being a word related to the gardens of monks. As the years passed, the word minch became corrupted to milch, thus Liebfraumilch. It is made from Sylvaner Riesling or Muller-Thurgau grapes, is mild and sweet, and is now an official Q.B.A. from Nahe, Rheingau, Rheinhessen and Rheinpfalz. As for Niersteiner, as already mentioned as a wine known in the 9th and 10th centuries, it comes from the 300 or so beautiful vineyards around the town of Nierstein on the Rhine itself. As in the upper Rhine area, most of the wines of Rheinhessen are made by cooperatives.

North of Mainz the Rhine swings westwards, and here, on the north bank is the Rheingau, another of the famous wine-producing regions. Indeed, from it come two of the best-known German wines, Johannisberg and Rudesheimer. The Johannisberg vineyards are a magnificent sight, formed in the shape of an amphitheatre and surmounted by the Schloss, or castle. There was a vineyard there in the 12th century, and the estate has a dramatic history in recent years, for it was given by Napoleon to one of his marshals; then at the Congress of Vienna to the Emperor of Austria, who gave it to the Von Metternick family, which still owns it. From its vineyards of Riesling grapes comes one of Germany's most distinguished wines, one that is imitated in many other countries, including the

United States. Rudesheim, some three miles downstream is by a steep mountain, and many of the vineyards have been formed by cutting terraces in its face, and on these is produced one of Germany's best-known wines. In neighbouring Geisenheim is a viticultural training college with a world-wide reputation. On the other side of Rudesheim is the town Assmannshausen which is exceptional in the Rheingau for producing red wine from the Pinot Noir grapes. Altogether, the Rheingau, with its 5500 acres of vineyards is probably the most distinguished of Germany's wine-growing areas, its wines being delicate and fresh with a strong bouquet.

So far we have stuck to the course of the Rhine, but at Bingen the great river is joined by a tributary, the Nahe, which itself flows through one of the wine-growing areas, and later, at Koblenz, by the Moselle, which flows through another and itself has two tributaries, the Ruwer and the Saar.

Let us consider the latter group first for Moselle is a wine of world-wide reputation. Before the river enters Germany it has flowed many miles from the Vosges mountains in France, but the vineyards which line its banks in France strangely enough produce only an indifferent wine. It is when the river has flowed some miles into Germany beyond Trier, where the banks become high, steep and slopy that the true Moselle wines are formed. Wine is produced along the river before then, but is indifferent and mainly for local consumption. But then starts a different story. For the next 40 miles or so the Moselle twists and turns like a snake, and on its banks are produced the famous Moselle wines such as Piesporter. Like Johannisberg, its vineyards at Piesport form a giant amphitheatre in tiers, and here is produced, among other wines, the unique Goldtrapfchen, sweet and fragrant. Then there is Braundeberg, first planted with grapes by the Romans. Then Bernkastel, chief town of the region, famous for its Doktor wines. Some eight miles further downstream at Urzig, the soil becomes more clayey, and the wine takes on a different flavour, and from then on the wines, though pleasant,

become more commonplace, for we have left the region of the great Moselle wines.

We have not mentioned the wines of the Saar and the Ruwer, the two tributaries of the Moselle. Like the whole of the Moselle area, the vineyards of the Saar region produce poor, indifferent and good wines. The best of the vineyards are at Wiltingen, where Scharzhof and Scharzberg wines are produced. Some experts claim that Scharzberg is among the world's greatest wines. Most important of the Ruwer area vineyards are those at Kasel and Eitelsbach.

Finally there is the Nahe region, surrounding the river of that name that enters the Rhine at Bingen. It is a beautiful area of valleys of rich agricultural land, broken up by orchards and vineyards. It produces slightly more wine than Rheingau on the opposite side of the Rhine, but the general quality is low. Nevertheless, the area produces some wine of great distinction. The area differs from most German regions in that it is planted with Sylvaner rather than Riesling grapes. Best-known of the region's wines are made at Bad, Kreuznach, and Schloss, Bockelheim.

There is so much more to be said about German wines that space does not permit. Like the simple fact that all, except those of Franconia, are bottled in long-neck shaped bottles (those of Franconia in flasks). Or the complicated naming of the official designated boundaries. But enough has been said in the foregoing pages to justify Germany's claim to be one of the world's leading wine countries.

Harvest time in a small German village. Typical scenery in German wine-producing districts includes the hillsides covered with terraced vineyards. **Left:** *St. Urban, Patron saint of wine.* **Above:** *Wooden casks stored in a German wine cellar.*

Italy

Until 20 years ago when the Italian government passed wine control laws, the wine situation in the country - the largest wine producer in the world, was somewhat chaotic. It was in 1963 that three official standards were introduced: Denominazione Semplice, Denominazione di Origine Controllata, and Denominazione Controllata e Guarantita. The first does not control any standards, merely stating in which region the wine originates; the second defines the area in which a particular wine may be produced, and lays down certain standards of quality. The trouble with the D.O.C. registrations is that they are mainly by small, individual concerns (there are 35 in Piedmont alone), so confusion is in danger of becoming more confounded. The last Denominazione names the wines of high quality from select zones which have been bottled by the producer who guarantee full responsibility - the bottles being sealed with a government seal.

In a country like Italy, with its huge variety of wines made from grapes often grown on small vineyards, and turned into wine by cooperatives it is best to approach the problem region by region, but in the back of the mind should always be a realisation of the climate Italy enjoys. Its southernmost point in Sicily is over 700 miles from the north where most of Italy's finest wines are produced, but wine is made through the whole length of the country from grapes grown in over four million acres of vineyards. In some, the vines are actually grown up trees bordering farms. The climate is generally warm to hot, moderated by the Mediterranean and Adriatic Seas, and the soil well-suited for vines, with the Alps in the north and the Appenines running the length of the country providing a good, stony basis in most areas. Piedmont in the north is approximately on the same latitude as Bordeaux, and Sicily on that of the sherry country of Spain.

Not only is Piedmont on the same latitude as Bordeaux, but it adjoins France, and, like Rioja in Spain, its winemakers may have come to be grateful for the fact. It is here that, south-west of Turin, we find two of Italy's greatest red wines, Barola, (up to 15% alcoholic strength), and Barbarescu, full and dark reds made from the Nebbiolu grape. Both age extremely well. From a few miles south comes another famous Italian wine, this time of the white, sparkling variety, sometimes called "poor man's champagne" - Asti Spumanti. Sweet and scented, and made from the Moscato grapes, it is usually made by the **Charmat** method (used widely in California) of making champagne, i.e. by bulk fermentation and bottling under pressure. Another noteworthy red wine, though not of the quality of Barola is Barbera, made from the grape of that name. But before leaving the Turin area we should not fail to mention its famous Vermouth which, although not a natural wine, must contain 70% of wine. The wines used are from the Moscato grapes, flavoured with aromatic herbs. The names of Cinzano and Martini of Turin are both world-famous.

Moving westward across the Lombardy plain, there are certainly plenty of wines - 40 or more could be named, but many varieties of the same wines, and none particularly outstanding. North of Milan coming along the banks of the River Adda are three very similar red wines of the Valtellina, one with the forbidding name of Inferno, the others Grumello and Sassella, (from the Nebbiolu grape) which are worthy of mention. Moving further west towards Trieste and Yugoslavia, the character of the wines seems to change, as do the grapes from which they are made. From near Verona comes what is, perhaps, Italy's best-known red wine - Valpolicella, light red in colour, and made from Corvina, Negrara, Molinara and Rondinella grapes. Nearby is Soave, known for its fine white wines made from Garganega grapes. Some 45 miles to the south in the region of Emilia-Romagna, the Lambrusco grape is used to make the wine of that name - an unusual wine indeed, for it is red, dry and sparkling, three qualities not normally found in combination: and on the other side of Bologna we get Albana, a popular white wine from the grape of the same name. Farther north, in the Alto-Adice, near the Austrian border, we find far more non-Italian grapes being used - Riesling, Sylvaner, Traminer, Pinot Noir, Sauvignon, and Merlot among them. Much of the wine from this area is exported, mainly to neighbouring Austria. Finally on our eastern journey across northern Italy we come to the area round Venice and Trieste and find the same wider use of foreign grapes, mostly the same as those listed above.

Continuing southwards to the neighbourhood of Florence and beyond, we come to perhaps the most famous of Italy's wine-producing regions - Tuscany. What would the vast majority of people say if asked quickly to name an Italian wine? The answer, of course, is Chianti. Apart from its other wines, which are many, Tuscany produces no less than 27,000,000 gallons of Chianti in a year. It is made from a blend of four grapes, Sangiovese, Trebbiano, Black Canaiolo, and Malvasia, and all but the very best are made by the Governo system of a second fermentation. Also, all but the very best are bottled in the familiar wicker-netted flasks, while the very best are bottled and aged in normal bottles. Although Chianti dominates the Tuscany scene, many other wines are produced there, and special mention should be made of one, Brunello Di Montallino, made from the grape Brunello, and said to be Italy's most expensive wine. To misquote Lord

Harvesting grapes in the Italian sun in the wine-growing area of Piedmont (the foot of the mountains) in the north where some of Italy's finest wines are produced.

The wine list

15·8·2015

Sicily is a fascinating fusion of different cultures – but the wines I have sampled have not lived up to expectations for a long time. Now I am pleased to see Sicily is fast becoming a European hotspot for brilliant bargain reds. I first visited the island 30 years ago, when Sicily was better known as a main supplier of bulk wine to the chillier north. I remember visiting a small handful of producers and being impressed by the wealth of native white and red grapes, but not by the quality of their rather rustic reds and inelegant whites.

Sicily has vast tracts of vineyards planted with their own fascinating native grapes, which have for years been channelled into those blends to bolster northern wines. Progress has been slow, but local wine producers, led by families like the Planetas in western Sicily, are now gaining confidence and have realised they have a treasure trove of native grapes which should be explored.

From the high altitude vineyards of Mount Etna, to the south coast around Syracuse and the windswept island of Pantelleria, Sicily has an amazing array of styles on offer. Most progress has been made with reds. Two varieties which stand out as offering fantastic value are nero d'avola and frappato – the king and queen of Sicilian red grapes.

Nero d'avola is the most widely planted red grape on the island. It is a muscular, masculine heavyweight among reds with a deep black red colour, high alcohol, sweet chocolate notes, firm tannins with plenty of ageing potential.

Frappato is one of my recent discoveries. It has such a fabulous freshness with vibrant acidity – a lighter style of wine – with a succulent strawberry flavour, floral, very fruity – pinot noir-like in its elegance but with a certain underlying pepperiness. It lives up to its name – meaning "fruitful" as it can smell and taste really grapey.

You can find both these varietal wines in UK wine merchants and supermarkets – at very attractive prices. Those we tasted were under £18, with most under £10.

"The latest Sicilian harvest in 2014 is one to watch," says Sebastian Payne of The Wine Society. "Whilst the rest of Italy had a very tricky 2014 vintage, the far south had a surprisingly good one."

CANTINE DI GAGGIANO

CHIANTI

CANTINE DI GAGGIANO

DENOMINAZIONE DI ORIGINE CONTROLLATA

0,75 ℓ

CONFEZIONATO DA

chianti Melini S.p.A.

GAGGIANO - ITALIA

11,8% VOL.

e

Macaulay, when a bottle of Brunello Di Montallino appears on the table "even the ranks of Tuscany can scarce forbear to cheer."

Farther south we come to the Lazio region of the capital, Rome, only a few miles south of which, on the Alban hills, known for its Castelli wines, the best-known being Frascati, a strong, fragrant, pale straw-coloured white wine, which can be dry, semi-sweet or sweet.

We are now getting down towards the toe, or rather **two** toes of Italy; into the really warm climate. In Campania near Naples, Vesuvia raises its historic head, and on its volcanic slopes grow Coda Di Volpe, Greco di Torre and Biancolella grapes, from which are made Lachryma Christi, a not very distinguished wine, but one known to many for what some regard as its slightly blasphemous name, which means the Tears of Christ. We are now down in the really hottest part of the country, and although huge quantities of wines are produced in both toes of the country, it is of coarse quality, and

used often for blending. Finally there is Sicily, whose most famous wine is Marsala, a fortified wine, some of which is made by the Solera system, as with sherry. It is a dessert wine, heavy and sweet and mixed with egg yolks and is used in making that favourite Italian sweet, Zabaglione.

The foregoing picture, it may be hoped, gives some idea of the extent of the confusion in the Italian wine scene. Although many of these are practically identical, there are hundreds of wine names, and almost, it seems, as many different grapes used in their manufacture. There are a few outstanding table wines, many, many more ordinary wines, most of them drunk locally, and a vast quantity used for blending and in the manufacture of Vermouth.

Below: The castle at Briolo, 20 miles south of Florence, where Baron Ricasoli devised the classic formula for Chianti which is still made there. Right: A rich harvest in Piedmont, in the region of Barola and Barbarescu.

Right: Vineyards at Pressano, Italy looking through vines which are high-trained in the pergola style. The Dolomites are in the background. Below: Harvesting grapes in Grignolino, in the Piedmonte region of Italy. No doubt the best-known wine produced in this region is the sparkling white wine, Asti Spumante. Gavi is one of the great wines of Italy produced in this area, and is made from the Cortese grape. Bottom: Terraced vineyards trail almost to the sea's edge.

An ingenious way to harvest grapes by a Spanish grower.
Many Spanish grapes are grown by smallholders and sold to
wineries where the wine is actually made.

THE WINES OF SPAIN
& PORTUGAL

Two of the best known wines - unusual because they are fortified and made quite differently from normal wines - come from the same area of Europe: the Iberian Peninsula. They are, of course, Sherry and Port, the first from Spain and the second from Portugal. Both countries produce other wines - indeed, Spain is one of the largest grape-growing countries in the world, but few people could readily name any other wine from either country. We shall try to help them later in this chapter, but first let us look at how sherry and port are made, taking sherry first.

It takes its name, of course, from the town of Jerez de la Frontera in the south of Spain about fifteen miles from Cadiz and seventy five from Gibraltar. The grapes used to make it are the Palomino, a local grape, and Pedro Ximenes, which are grown in many Spanish vineyards. The feature of the best vineyards in which the Palomino is grown is the fine chalky nature of the soil, and it is from these that the finos, the basis of most sherries, are made. Grapes from the less chalky, more sandy vineyards, are more prolific. Rainfall is moderate and there are months of Spanish sunshine to ripen the grapes, which are harvested round about the middle of September.

The grapes are crushed as usual to make must, the first and second pressings going straight into special semi-porous oak butts, which are left in the sun for a time to speed up fermentation, then moved to the bodegas, where the wine is made. They remain there until January so that, aided by the semi-porous nature of the butts which allows oxygen to reach the wine, a mould called flor forms on the top. This process continues for three or four months, when the wine is racked and given a fortification of around 2% of grape spirit. There follows a longer period of fermentation, after which the wine is racked again and the Solera system of blending begun. The Solera system depends on maintaining a chain of sherries of different ages so that each year two things happen. First, the new sherry can be blended with other similar new sherries; secondly the required amount of the oldest sherry is drawn off for use and replaced by the next oldest in the chain, and so on down the line.

The finest of the sherries are the finos, pale and dry. Amontillado, darker and slightly sweeter, may have started its wine life as a fino which had been left in the butt for a long time, but quite deliberately Amontillado grapes are picked slightly earlier. From the coastal area about twenty miles north west of Jerez comes Manzanilla, fine and dry. Oloroso, made mainly from Palomino grapes, is made sweet by the addition of alcohol before fermentation is complete and has a high alcoholic content.

Spain's other wines are dealt with later in this chapter. Meanwhile, let us turn to the other special Iberian wine, Port. Its name, of course, derives from

Working in the cellars in a Spanish vineyard. Note the extended spigot from the top barrel for ease of drawing off the

the port of Oporto on the Atlantic coast, but it originates in the Alto Douro, about fifty miles to the north. It is in the Alto Douro that the actual wine is made. Like sherry and, for that matter, champagne, port is a blended wine made from a variety of different grapes which are crushed (sometimes still by foot) and then allowed to ferment until the sugar content is about 10%. At this stage, the fortification takes place, the must being transferred to casks containing enough brandy to stop further fermentation. The wine is then moved, sometimes by sailing boat, to Oporto, where it is blended and stored in warehouses called lodges. The special long one hundred and fifteen gallon barrels in which the wine is stored are called pipes. Length of storage depends very much on the type of Port involved, but it is rarely less than two or three years and may last for decades before or after bottling.

There are several types of Port, the most distinguished being Vintage Port - the wine of an exceptional year which requires little or no blending and which is bottled after two years, but perhaps not drunk for another twenty. Then there is Crusted Port, a blend of high quality wine. This, too, is bottled early for laying down and gets its name from the light sediment which forms during the maturing process. Tawny Port is so called because it has faded in colour from the rich red of the wine through lengthy maturing in the wood. Ruby Port is darker and less smooth than the others, being aged for only about two years. There is also, of course, White Port, made from white grapes but drunk as an aperitif and not as a dessert wine.

The great miracle of Port is its origin in the Alto Douro, which man has converted from a rocky wilderness into fruitful vineyards. Rising from the Douro River are now terraced vineyards, some dating back to the seventeenth century and with fifteen feet high walls. So steep and rough is the going that most of the grapes have to be manhandled down to the river level thousands of feet below.

contents. Spain is one of the largest grape-growing countries in the world, and is most famous for its sherries.

Other Wines
of Spain

As with Portuguese wines, few Spanish wine names other than Sherry are known abroad, although Spain has had its own version of the French Appellation Contrôlée system for years. Jerez, of course, is one of the designated areas and the other chief quality regions are Rioja, Montilla and Catalonia. The Rioja region lies along the Ebro River near Burgos in northern Spain and is particularly beautiful with gentle hills and the Sierra de Cantabria in the north. It has a long wine history, and as far back as the sixteenth century had its own form of Appellation Contrôlée. Generally speaking, the wines of Spain are strong and on the rough side, but those of Rioja have been strongly influenced by winemakers from Bordeaux, which is not that far away. When Phylloxera struck the Bordeaux area towards the end of the nineteenth century, many French wine growers moved into Northern Spain and they left a legacy of French wine-making methods there. The soil is chalky and the winters cold but not devastatingly harsh, while the summers are hot. As is usual in Spain, the grapes are grown in small vineyards and include the Rhône grape, Grenache. They are sold to the winemakers, who make and store the wine in the bodegas or warehouses similar to those used in the making of Sherry. Rioja wines may be white or red, although the red is usually the best. The Rioja area has three main zones: Rioja Alto (high), the most westerly with Haro as its centre; Rioja Alavesa and Rioja Baja, where the cheaper wines are produced. Among the better known bodegas are those of Frederico Paternina at Ollauri and the Compania Vinicola del Norte de España in Haro, which produces among others a dry white Monopole and a red Imperial. A feature of the Rioja wines is the length of time they are kept in the wood before bottling.

One of the largest wine-growing areas is La Mancha, south of Madrid, at the southernmost tip of which is the town of Valdapenas, and most of the strong wine of the area, which is drunk while young, is known by this name. As in Rioja, the red wines of most of the district except Valdapenas, where the Cencibal grape is used, are made from the Garnacha (Grenache) grape, while the white wines are made from the Airen and Vidoncha variety. Between La Mancha and the Mediterranean lie two other important wine-growing areas: Utier-Requena and Valencia, producing heavier and sweeter wines than La Mancha. Further north on the Mediterranean coast is Catalonia, from which comes Tarragona, a sweet red wine with high alcoholic content,

Priorato, mainly for blending with other wines. Then there is Panades, which yields a wine akin to sherry, as well as Vina Sol, a dry white, and Coronas, a heavy red. In the south of Spain to the east of Jerez there are two other significant wine areas - Montilla and Morilas - whose wine enjoys great popularity in Spain but are little known elsewhere.

The last is, in fact, true of the majority of Spanish wines except, of course, for the notable exception of Sherry. A good deal is exported purely for blending purposes, but the great majority is produced for home consumption and is unknown outside the area in which it is produced.

Below: Dao wines are produced in the granite hills of the area of Portugal just south of the River Douro. The quality of Portuguese wines is protected by an official body, The Fereacao which has affixed this seal to a vat of maturing Dao. Right: Mateus Rosé is perhaps, after Port and Madeira, the best-known Portuguese wine. The picture shows centrifugal equipment for clearing the wine which is produced in the modern winery, Sogrape, at Anadia in the north of the country. Below right: The "lodge" of Delaforce Sons and Ca in Vila Nova de Gaia, a suburb of Oporto where port is being matured after being brought down from the hilly vineyards and wineries of the Alto Douro. The area represents a remarkable human achievement for it consists of steep slate and granite slopes which had to be terraced and covered with soil. Some of the terraces are over two centuries old.

Fruit and oak to match game

RIOJA

BY SARAH JANE EVANS
MW
WINES FROM RIOJA

> **classic pairing of its delicate red fruit overlaid by fine oak**

As autumn draws in, our tastes seek something warmer and richer, in both food and rink. The delicious game terrine recipe given here will be delicious served with crusty bread and an elegant Gran Reserva Rioja.

The classic pairing of its delicate red fruit overlaid by fine oak will bring out the sweetness of the game, and balance the richness.

Gran Reserva wines are selected wines from exceptional vintages which have spent at least two years in oak casks and three years in the bottle. For white wines, the minimum ageing period is four years, with at least one year in casks.

Rioja wines are protected by the oldest Designation of Origin in Spain, officially recognised in 1926. In 1991, it was awarded the highest category – Calificada – making Rioja the only designation in Spain to be so honoured.

The first recognition of Rioja wines, however, came in 1102 when King Sancho of Navarra legally recognised the wines. The Royal Economic Society Rioja Growers, was created in 1787, aimed at promoting the cultivation of vines, wine production and trade development

25.9.2015

Other Wines of Portugal

One other of the many wines of Portugal has a worldwide reputation and a history of its own. This is Madeira, once the fashionable wine of the nineteenth century both in England and the United States. It is a fortified wine like Port. The island from which it takes its name lies in the Atlantic some five hundred miles from the coast of Morocco and with its terraced vineyards has some similarity with the Alto Douro. There are four main varieties of grape used to make Malmsey, a rich sweet dark brown wine, or Bual, slightly drier, both desert wines; Verdelho and Sercial - the former usable either as a aperitif or as a dessert wine, and the latter, for the Sercial grape is the German Riesling, an excellent aperitif.

Portugal produces one distinguished table wine, Mateus Rosé, in Vila Real in the Douro area, but the main areas for its other wines are Minho, from Oporto to the Spanish frontier in the north and west, and Dao, some seventy miles further south. The wines from the Minho area, although called vinho verde - green wine - are mainly red and are slightly petillant. Those produced in the Dao area are rather ordinary reds and whites.

*Left: Harvesting grapes in the Minho area of Portugal where the vines are frequently trailed overhead. The vino verde wines, produced in the mountainous area bordering the Atlantic, young and fresh, are in contrast to the rich ports produced in the neighbouring Douro. **Above:** An ancient wine press preserved at a Portuguese wine lodge.*

California is by no means the only wine producing state in the U.S.A. to introduce modern techniques and machinery. Here at the Warner Vineyards in Paw Paw, Michigan a mechanised harvester gathers in the year's crop.

THE WINES OF
THE USA

The feature of the wine scene in North America today is the rapidity with which it is changing. Wine has been produced there since the Jesuit fathers introduced the Mission grape into California at the end of the 17th century, and nearly a century earlier the British Governor of Virginia brought vines over from England. As in France and elsewhere in Europe the church played an important part in laying the foundations of California's wine industry. At one time all the vineyards of California were attached to the Jesuit missions, not only for the production of sacramental wines but, no doubt, for the delectation of the missioners and others. But all this was to change - California was part of Mexico, which was a Spanish colony, so that when Mexico lost the war against the United States in 1847 California became the 31st state of the Union. All these changes affected the wine scene.

Under Mexican rule a few Europeans and Americans developed vineyards but under United States rule the real seeds of the present vast wine industry of the State were sown. New settlers moved in from the East, especially new European immigrants whose traditional drink was wine. By the 1860's many of California's famous wine names were already established and flourishing and the names of the Napa and Sonoma valleys becoming known. But there were to be serious setbacks. The vine disease devastated many of its vineyards. As had happened in Europe (also struck by the disease) the Californian grape growers grafted on Eastern American root stocks (which had become immune to the disease) but all this took time. Then a second, this time manmade disaster struck. The United States Government introduced Prohibition, and in common with the rest of the country California's grapes were supposed to be used only for eating or for non-alcoholic and sacramental wine made under licence. The immediate result, of course, was disastrous. Many vineyards disappeared or were changed to other crops, wine-making equipment etc. was sold off. As will be shown later the years of Prohibition did eventually bring some benefit to California, but that is another story.

It must be emphasised that although California goes unchallenged as the major wine-producing state wines had been produced in many other places for centuries - in, for example, Michigan, Ohio, and particularly in New York State in the Finger Lake area and the Hudson River valley.

The difficulty with American wine was that it was not very palatable to European taste - nor, for that matter, to sophisticated American taste either.

Warner Brothers of Paw Paw, Michigan believe in traditional methods as much as they do in modern techniques. They pride themselves on their many cask wines matured in the wood and they certainly do not stint themselves when it comes to the size of the casks.

There were plenty of vines and grapes - after all Lief Ericsson when he reached America in about A.D. 1000 named it Vinland because of the abundance of vines. The trouble was that the native American grapes belong to the **Vitis labrusca** and **Vitis rotundifola** families which tend to make "foxy", rather sour wines, while the European grapes are of the **Vitis Vinifera** family, capable of producing smoother and more subtle varieties. California and New York had been experimenting with European vine stock but most of this was halted by Prohibition. In the long term this brought some advantages. With repeal American wine growers left in the game did two things - one was to plant up much more European stock, the other to take advantage of scientific developments and new wine making methods. The State University of California opened its famous Department of Viticulture and Enology at Davis, an institution which enjoys high prestige not only in the United States but in Europe and elsewhere.

American native grapes include: Catawba, Concord, perhaps the best known, Delaware, Dutchess, Ives, Niagara, Scuppernong, but the grapes mostly used in modern American wines are of European origin especially Cabernet Sauvignon, Chardonnay, Chenin Blanc, Gamay, Gewurtztraminer, Grenache, Merlot, Muller-Thurgau, Muscat, Pinot Noir, Riesling, Semillon, Sylvaner, Syrah and Zinfandel.

A consequence of this is that where in France, for example, particular types of wines are associated with a district eg. Côtes du Rhône, St. Emilion etc., in the United States they may be produced almost anywhere. Thus Washington produces its Cabernet Sauvignon as do Californian wineries. Idaho, Oregon and others all produce Johannisberg Riesling and, of course, many states including New York produce Champagne sometimes by the méthode Champenoise, sometimes not.

California is, of course, by far the largest of the wine states, some eight times the vineyard acreage of the next largest, New York, followed by Washington, Michigan, Pennsylvania and Ohio, but the list of wine-growing states is increasing almost daily with the opening of vineyards small in size but grand in ambition. Some have already achieved distinction and the French wine world was rocked in 1980 when at a blind-tasting of French and American wines in Paris the second prize went to a 1975 Pinot Noir from the Eyrie vineyard in Oregon. It was scarcely second prize for the winner was a 1959 Chambelle Musigny which scored 70 points. The American Pinot Noir scored 69.8, beating a Chambertin, Beaune & Vosne - Romanée. Even Virginia now has a score of vineyards and wineries producing Rieslings, Merlots, Cabernet Sauvignon, Gewurtztraminer etc. It must be said again that most of them are small, and most untried, but they are there and they are a sign of the future.

California. There is really nothing like California in the world wine scene. There are the giants of the industry like Paul Masson (owned by the Seagram Company) with a storage capacity of 23 million gallons using the grapes from thousands of acres of vineyards: or E. J. Gallo of Modesto, S. California using grapes from 100,000 acres of vineyards with a capacity of 2,000,000 gallons of wine and modern stainless steel and glass storage tanks that have been compared to a Middle East oil depot: or the Italian Swiss colony capable of producing 8,000,000 gallons. These and other giants, of course, aim at the popular market and most of their wines are very ordinary but they also make for the more sophisticated market. Paul Masson's for example, have a distinguished Pinnacles selection including Chardonnay and Johannisberg Riesling and Gewurtztraminer and Fumé Blanc.

California, with over 3,000 vineyards and wineries has its climatic peculiarities, and the Department of Viticulture and Enology has divided it into five zones on the basis of the temperatures during the grape-growing periods each year. The result is that although the hottest region might be expected to be in the South, behind Los Angeles similar temperatures are experienced much further north. Two famous wine growing areas are the Sonoma and Napa valleys north of San Francisco, and there some of the famous, indeed historic wineries are to be found, such as the Buena Vista Winery (620 acres), the Christian Brothers (600 acres), Louis M. Martini (900 acres) and so on, but it should be remembered that the size of the vineyards may well be misleading for many wineries make their wine from grapes from other growers. Another feature of the modern American wine scene is the search for micro-climates. These are areas, often quite small, where because of sheltered position, soil, climatic conditions certain grapes will grow successfully but could fail in the general surrounding area.

South of San Francisco is the Salinas area, separated from another wine-growing area by the

CHATEAU ESPERANZA

1980
Aurora Blanc

NEW YORK STATE
Alcohol 10% by Volume

SMITH VINEYARDS

500 Cases Produced and Bottled by
CHATEAU ESPERANZA, Bluff Point, NY 14417
Bonded Winery #663

Joaquin Valley.

It is quite impossible to name all American wines. There are, of course, the local names that strike Europeans as peculiar. These include such agreeable fantasies as Cold Duck, even Very Cold Duck, Hot Rumour, Love My Goat, Eye of the Partridge, Moodie Blue and Lonesome Charlie. But most American wines are now sold under the name of the grape from which they are made. These are called varietals, and the label shows the winery from which they come, sometimes the name of the vineyard and the alcoholic content. Thus one label chosen at random says: "1979 Napa Zinfandel, 100% Zinfandel grapes from the Mt. Veeden area of Napa County. Produced and bottled by Gius Zeffoni & Norman C de Leuza, Napa, California. Alcohol 13% by volume". On another example "Chateaux Esperanza 1980 AURORA BLANC New York State Alcohol 10% by volume. Smith Vineyards. 500 cases produced and bottled by Chateau Esperanza etc." It will be noticed that where in Europe the wine would almost certainly have a geographical name such as St. Julien or St. Estelle, here it has the name of the grape from which it is made. Aurora Blanc is a Franco-American hybrid grape.

California presents a very mixed picture in more respects than one. There are the small wineries, often family run, and sometimes producing wines of high quality - the Americans call high quality wines premium wines; there are the newcomers as has been said small but ambitious: and the giants of the business, some still privately-owned such as E&J Gallo, and others, like Paul Masson, which is a subsidiary of the Seagram Company. There are small concerns with distinguished reputations such as the Schramsberg Vineyards, 120 years old, with only 40 acres of its own, noted for its champagne

The broad expanse of the Lawrence Winery Vineyards in California. California is well-known as America's foremost wine-producing state, its 300 or more vineyards and wineries producing more than 400,000,000 gallons of wine each year.

made by the méthode champenoise, which is drunk at the White House, and was even taken to Peking by President Nixon for official receptions. Or the Christian Brothers in Napa Valley, a Roman Catholic religious teaching order whose profits after tax go to help finance their teaching and religious activities, and who have a storage capacity of 9,500,000 gallons. Their wines include Brut - Extra-Dry Champagne, Cabernet Sauvignon, Chardonnay, Napa Fumé and Zinfandel. There are few wineries that do not produce as many or more varieties: Massons produce 47 types of table, dessert, aperitif and sparkling wine as well as brandy. There lies the difference between wine production, for example, in France.

Although California is best known for its white wines of the Napa and Sonoma valleys, many wineries produce red wines including Cabernet Sauvignon, Pinot Noir and particularly Zinfandel. Leading varietals among the white are Pinot Chardonnay, Pinot Blanc, Johannisberg Riesling, Semillon and Gewurtztraminer. Interestingly, while Federal regulations require that when a wine is labelled with a grape name 75% of the grapes must come from the district named on the label, California requires that in any wine labelled as coming from California, 100% must be from that state.

But California is not the only Pacific coast state in the wine business. Oregon, the next state to the north has come into the picture in the last decade or so, the acreage of vineyards having increased from 85 acres in 1970 to 2500 in 1983, while wineries increased from 7 to 30. Mention has already been made of the 1980 triumph in Paris of the Oregon Pinot Noir by the eighteen year old Eyrie vineyards. Even more remarkable has been the development of the most northerly of the western states - Washington. Twenty years ago it had no vineyards and no wineries. Today it has 4000 acres planted with vinifera grapes and a score of more wineries. It is now the third largest grape growing state in the Union although, of course, not all the grapes go to make wine. Here again, a wide range of varieties is produced. Take, for example, the Château St. Michelle in the Yakima Valley. It gathered its first harvest from its 750 acres in 1967 and its wines include Chardonnay, Cabernet Sauvignon, Chenin Blanc, Johannisberg Riesling, Merlot, and a Blanc de Noir made by the méthode champenoise.

New York State goes unchallenged as the second most important wine state, with 40,000 acres of vineyards. There are three main growing areas, that of the Finger Lakes more or less in the centre of the state: the Erie Chautauqua strip along the coast of Lake Erie in the west: and the Hudson River Valley in the east. Most important of these is the Finger Lakes area named after the five lakes which have the shape of the five fingers of a hand. Glacial in origin, the lakes are just south of Lake Ontario. The sloping banks, strong and well-drained, provide admirable soil for the vineyards, and the lakes themselves help to moderate the temperature. At one time, only American native grapes were used in the wines of the

district, but in recent years, under the leadership of Charles Fournier (once winemaker of the famous French champagne firm Veuve Clicquot) and later Dr. Konstantin Frank, encouraged the introduction of European vinifera stock - something thought previously to be impossible. However, the bulk of New York State wine is still made from home American grapes.

Outstanding is Gold Seal Vineyard Inc. at Hammondsport, noted for its Gold Seal Champagnes, but which produces also gold Seal Cold Duck (a mixture of Burgundy and Champagnes) and among others Catawba Reds and Whites from the American Catawba grape. Another well-known and distinguished winery is the Taylor Wine Company, just over a century old, and today owned by the Coca-Cola company. It is one of the largest producers of bottle-fermented sparkling wines in the world. Its Lake County wines are all from Franco - American hybrid grapes. Other wineries in the area include Widmers producing, among a wide variety of wines Crackling Lake Niagara Champagne, and Pink Catawba, both from native American grapes, as well as Pale Dry Sherry and Tawny Port; the Great Western winery, also owned by Coca-Cola, renowned for its Great Western Champagne for over a century, and one of the few American wineries to use the Solera system (see Spain) in making Sherry.

More than a half of the vineyards of New York State are situated in the Erie-Chautauqua region along the east coast of Lake Erie from the Niagara area in the north to the Pennsylvania state line in the south. Here, the majority of grapes grown are American native, including Delaware, Concord, Catawba and Niagara, but there is a strong movement towards replacements by European hybrids. It is not surprising, therefore, that the all-over wine list of the area, as it were, includes American Chablis, Chautauqua Niagara, Maréchal Foch, Johannisberg Riesling, Pinot Chardonnay, Dutchess Sauterne, Chardonnay,

Gewurtztraminer, Cabernet Sauvignon and Champagne.

Left: Many American wineries are quite small and are family run businesses owing their origins to ancestors who produced wine in Europe. The Boskydel Vineyards and Winery at Lake Leelenau on Lake Michigan is one of them. Part of its 25 acres is shown here. The great-grandfather of the founder grew grapes along the Mosell River and son and grandson did the same after immigration in Ohio. Right: All the family, including the proprietor's wife as is common in the smaller American wineries rally round at harvest time. Here one of the sons is gathering the crop. The grapes grown are French-American hybrids combining the wine quality of French vine with the disease resistant American roots. The winery produces Johannisberg Riesling, de Chaunac, red and rosé wines, Seyval Blanc and others. Michigan is the fourth largest wine producing state in the U.S.A.

The Hudson River Valley region is in the east of New York State just north of New York City between the Appallachian Mountains and the Catskills. It was once one of the countries oldest wine areas but suffered an eclipse during Prohibition, barely surviving. In recent years there have been distinct signs of a revival with eight of its dozen or so wineries having started only since 1960. In fact the oldest operating winery in the U.S. is the Brotherhood Winery of Washingtonville, which produced its first wine in 1839. It survived Prohibition, and despite its name, since 1978 became owned and run by one of the first woman winemakers in the U.S. It gets its grapes from its own vineyards, but buys too from vine growers throughout the state. As well as the normal wines, it produces what are called special wines including May Wine - a light white wine "with woodruff herbs, strawberry, and other natural flavours added".

There is one winery in this area calling for special mention - the Benmar wine Co. in Marlboro, for it is a combination of experimental station providing enological and viticulture data, sponsored by the Société des Vignerons, and a working winery. The produce of the working winery, especially the best, is supplied to the members of the Société des Vignerons. The work of the experimental station is designed to help the revival of the wine industry of the Hudson River Valley region.

Other Wine States: Michigan: This state ranks fourth in the wine making list of states with 12,500 acres of vineyards mostly concentrated at the southern end of Lake Michigan, but with some at the northern end. Of its 15 wineries, only 6 existed before 1970 - another example of the recent growth of the wine industry in the U.S. One of the oldest, the Bronte Champagne Wine Co. of Detroit, has a storage capacity of 1,000,000 gallons and produces not only the normal range of red and white wines, but sweet sherry, Port and vermouth. One of the youngest, Fenn Valley Vineyards and Wine Cellar of Fennville, has only six regular employees (with outside labour engaged for harvesting and pruning) and the vineyard with a storage capacity of 60,000 gallons grows only European vinifera grapes. The St. Julian Wine Co. in Paw Paw, with storage capacity of 1,500,000 gallons, has also, in recent years, moved over to Franco-American hybrid grapes most of which it buys from local growers. Also in Paw Paw is the Warner Valley Vineyard and Winery which produces premium wines of repute, champagne by the methode champenoise, and more unusual, sherry and port by the **Solera** system. Michigan has one somewhat dubious claim to fame. It is that it invented Cold Duck, a combination of American Burgundy and Champagne that is popular throughout the country. Neighbouring

Ohio is another state signalling the growing interest in the revival of wine production, with some 25 new wineries established in the last twenty years. They are all along the southern shore of Lake Erie, and include Ohio's best known winery, Meier's Wine Cellars Inc., where 350 acres of vineyards on Bass Island in the lake provide them with 1500 to 2000 tons of grapes annually. Here, too, a switch over from the traditional native American to **vinifera** grapes is taking place. **Virginia,** which had a reputation for claret in the 19th century, and then disappeared from the wine scene, has also returned to the fray with a score of new vineyards ranging from 4½ to 45 acres in size. All being new vineyards,

their production consists almost entirely of vinifera or Franco-American hybrid grapes with the familiar list of Johannisberg Riesling, Cabernet Sauvignon, Chardonnay, Merlot, Gewurtztraminer, Pinot Noir etc, the final result.

Wine, of course, is produced in other states, but in very modest quantities, and mainly for local consumption. An outstanding exception is the Boordy Vineyard Inc. in Hydes, Maryland, founded by Philip Wagner, an American authority on wine. Wine is made in Pennsylvania, Vermont, on Long Island, in the Carolina's and, no doubt, in many other states, but for practical purposes in the world wine scene, it is California and its Pacific neighbours, New York, Ohio and Michigan that count.

Growing grapes on the Isle St. George, on Lake Erie. The island once belonged to Canada, and is now called Bass Island, but the vineyards which still grow grapes there still use the name Ile St. George on their wine labels. This vineyard is owned by Meier's Wine Cellars, who are the largest producers of wine in the state of Ohio, and who have been in business for over 100 years. The wine industry was first brought to Ohio by the Moravian missionaries working with the Delaware Indians.

1981 Maryland Dry White Wine

TABLE WINE PRODUCED AND BOTTLED BY BOORDY VINEYARDS, HYDES, MD. 21082 BW-MD-29 · THE R. B. DEFORD FAMILY, PROPS.

Boordy Vineyards ★ Established 1945

Working in the Meredyth Vineyards Virginia, whose vines combine the heritage of both the old and the new worlds.

A rich harvest from this sunny vineyard in the Barossa Valley in South Australia. The valley with its vineyards, orchards and olive groves was pioneered by German immigrants in the middle of the nineteenth century and produces quality wines from quality grapes.

THE WINES OF AUSTRALIA
& SOUTH AFRICA

Australia: In 1788 Captain Arthur Philip arrived in Australia to establish the colony of New South Wales, and became its first governor. As soon as his house was built he sent for vines for his garden, and so may be said to have been the father of Australia's wine industry, although there is no evidence that he made wine with the grapes. However there is no doubt that soon early settlers started small vineyards on their own. By 1803 the local paper was advising settlers how to plant vineyards, and in 1827 one of them actually won a silver medal, and six years later a gold medal in London for wine he had grown in the Parrammata Valley. Since then an industry has developed which has made Australia a considerable figure on the wine scene, producing some 113,000,000 gallons annually, of which about two-thirds are table wines.

Although the recent history of wine in Australia is very similar to that of the United States, nothing could be more different than that of the past two centuries. Australia had no phylloxera - or very little - and no Prohibition to check development. Only comparatively recently has the widespread introduction of European vine stock developed widely in the United States, whereas Australian grapes are all descended from the original European vines or new vineyards planted only with stock from Europe. As far back as the 1830's some vineyards close to Melbourne were planted up with Château Haut Brion, and the names of Australian wines reveal their origins - Rhine Riesling, Chardonnay, Merlot, Traminer, Cabernet Sauvignon, Shiraz, to pick a few at random. Where Australian and American wine history has begun to coincide in recent years is in changing taste which is being met by changing production. In earlier years both countries had a reputation for fairly hard drinking. Only 20 years ago, out of just over 42 million gallons of wine production in Australia, only about 15% was dry or sweet table and sparkling wine: 25% fortified wines, and the rest was distilled. But developing taste for table wines, and those of a lighter, dryer character at that brought about dramatic changes. Fourteen years later, table wines outnumbered fortified wines by more than two to one, with white wines 50% higher than red, when, previously, two red bottles had been sold for every one white. As a consequence more Australian wine is today sold abroad, and more drunk at home. The growth in popularity of dryer white wines has, of course, influenced the winemakers to take advantage of new scientific developments, especially in the field of refrigeration, and to turn towards white grapes. Riesling and Gewurztraminer have proved highly appreciative of Australian conditions.

Not unnaturally, most of the Australian wine-producing areas are where heat is not too excessive, which excludes most of the country. In fact, only three growing areas are significant - New South Wales, where it all began, Victoria, and South Australia. Best known of the New South Wales districts is the Hunter Valley, farthest north of the good vineyards, where vineyards were planted up as early as 1828. Semillon is the white grape that flourishes there, Shiraz the red. Penfold's (Dalwood) and Lindeman's are the biggest wine firms in the area. Dalwood's north-east of Branxton was first planted in 1828 by winemaking veteran George Wyndham. The estate is now much larger than it was then since 700 acres were added in 1960 and planted with the top table wine varieties in orderly rows each nearly a mile long. Penfold's are renowned for their claret, especially Grand Hermitage, made from Hermitage or Shiraz grapes, and their Rhine Riesling which, rather confusingly, is made from Semillon grapes. More recently, near Griffith, some 300 miles to the south-west from the Hunter River Valley, the firm of McWilliams, using irrigation from the Murrumbrigee River have started producing excellent white wines using modern methods, and reds too. Other Hunter Valley wineries of distinction are Tyrrells and Rothbury estate.

It was mentioned earlier that Australia suffered very little from phylloxera at the end of the 19th century. It was, in fact, the neighbouring state of Victoria, to the south-west that took the brunt. Before the disease struck, Victoria was by far the biggest wine-producing state of the Commonwealth. Today it produces only 15% of the total produced in the whole country. One of its present most distinguished wineries, 100 miles or so west of Melbourne, is Seppelt's whose vineyards at Great Western produce the best of Australia's equivalent of champagne, which is known as Great Western (no relation to the champagne of New York State of the same name). Seppelt's also produce good red and other white wines including a Cabernet Sauvignon. Victoria also boasts a Château vineyard - the "château" being a timber-framed building rather like a New England chapel, surrounded by mulberries. This is Château Tanbilk, in the Goulbourn Valley, known for its Shiraz wines, and Chardonnay. Another well-known wine-producing area is Rutherglen - Corowa on the New South Wales border, famous for a liqueur made with Muscat grapes.

Last of the three important wine states is South Australia. It produces some of Australia's best wines, and has six wine producing areas, three of them virtually surrounding the State Capital, Adelaide. Most famous of the six is the Barossa Valley, with 22,000 acres of vineyards, many of them small, others large, such as Seppeltsfield, where Seppelt's (see Victoria) have their main vineyards, winery and distillery at Gramps Yalumba, Penfold's and others all producing

quality reds and whites. South Australia, whose wine industry was developed by German immigrants produces quality wines from quality grapes.

Left and below: Grapes grown in the Barossa Valley, in South Australia, which is probably the most well-known of the Australian wine-growing areas. Its climate is both hotter and drier than that of the traditional wine-producing regions in Europe, and more closely resembles that of Portugal rather than that of France or Germany. The Barossa Valley vines have escaped the ravages of **phylloxera,** *or "vine louse" which infests the leaves and roots of the vines, and which has caused massive destruction in both European and other Australian vineyards in the past. The techniques for wine-growing were first brought to the area by Silesian Lutherans who fled religious persecution because they refused to annex their church to the state church. Johann Gramp in 1847 planted the first vines in the Barossa Valley. Joseph Seppelt came from Germany and originally intended to grow tobacco but quickly turned his attention to growing grapes. He founded the House of Seppelt.*

The elegant estate of Groot Constantia in Cape Province,
South Africa which once produced a dessert wine named
Constantia rivalling the best in Europe. Now a museum it still
produces wine.

South Africa

If you look at the neck of a bottle of South African wine, you will see what looks like a complicated, multi-coloured label. It is, in fact, the government seal, equivalent of the provisions of the French Appellation Contrôlée law, but much more informative. It is printed both in Afrikaans and English - the English version being on the right-hand side of the seal, which can be crossed by up to four coloured horizontal strips. The whole purpose is to certify the truth, or guarantee what is on the label, the top blue strip confirming the place of origin; the second, red, guaranteeing the vintage; the third, green, confirms the cultivar or grape used; and, finally, a white strip attests that the wine is of superior quality according to the standards of the Wine and Spirit Board. The letters and figures printed vertically in the centre panels are official identification numbers.

The seals were introduced in 1972, when wine control legislation was passed to protect the consumer. The legislation named all production units - which are divided up into 51 estates, 14 wards consisting of groups of estates, 11 districts and 5 regions, the latter being combinations of districts. All of them lie in Cape Province in the Valley of the Olifants River Mountains, the Cedanburg, Drakenstein and Hex River Mountains, and the Langeberg Range. Vineyards cover some 170,000 acres and the grapes or cultivars principally grown are Cabernet Sauvignon, Pinotage, Shiraz,

Sylvaner, Palomino, Chenin Blanc, and Muscat d'Alexandrie, Pinot Noir and Cinsault, which is called Hermitage. The wine areas produce over 6 million hectolitres of wine each year.

Paarl, on approximately the same southern latitude as Jerez in spain's northern is the centre of the best sherry and port production, and South African sherry, although an imitation, is well-liked, both inside and outside the country. As in Spain, the sherry is made by the solera system. South African port is not so well known outside the country as its sherry, but centuries ago the Union produced one of the world's greatest desert wines, Constantia. Constantia lies on the southern outskirts of Cape Town, and although the secrets of its red wine have been lost, the present estate of Groot Constantia, now owned by the government, still makes outstanding red table wines, including Herrenrood, made from blended grapes, and Pinotage, made from a cross-breed grape from Cuisant and Pinot Noir.

Paarl and Stellenbosch are also the centres of the best table wine-producing area of the coastal region. The 400 acre vineyard of the Backsberg Estate Winery in Paarl valley among its many wines of Origin-Superior produces a significant Cabernet Sauvignon, and a highly-regarded Pinotage, and the Fairview Estate on Paarl Mountain an excellent Cabernet Sauvignon. The Vergenoego Estate in the Stellenbosch wine of origin area also has a fine Cabernet Sauvignon and a Shiraz among its many outstanding wines.

South Africa is also a big brandy producing country, and much of the wine it makes is used for this purpose. The vineyards of the Little Karoo, stretching from the Drakenstein Range to the Swetburg Mountains, with their loose, well-drained soil and hot summers, produce much of the wine for distillation, but also yield the sweet dessert wines and some of the strong red table wines. Brandy is stored for a minimum of three years in French oak casks, top brandies for five or ten years. Mention should also be made of South Africa's special liqueur, Van der Hum, one of the many cordials, vermouths etc. produced in the country, and certainly the best. It is a brandy flavoured with Naatjie, a type of tangerine.

Insert: South Africa is known both for its dessert and table wines and many of the former are produced in the areas of Paarl and Stellenbosch. Control over the quality, marketing and pricing of all wines in the Union is exercised by the KWV - the Kooperative Wijnbouwers Vereeniging von Zuid-Afrika. Picture shows 2,500 gallon blending vats in the main cellar of the cooperative at Paarl. Right: Harvesting in the Stellenbosch area which produces some fine wines. Note the typical architecture of the winery reminiscent of the facades of houses in Holland. Stellenbosch is known for its table wines, Paarl for its sherries.

*Preparing for the vintage in Georgia in the Soviet Union.
Among the wines produced in Georgia are two heavy reds and
shampanskoa which party goers will recognise as Champagne.*

USSR

Let us start with the Iron Curtain countries of Europe:

The Soviet Union has well over three million acres of vineyards running from Moldavia by the Black Sea to Georgia, Armenia and Azerbaijan. Under the control regulation, the wines they produce are in three categories - ordinary, named (place of origin, matured) and Kollektsionya (from selected grapes in selected areas and a minimum of two years maturing in bottles). Wines from Moldavia include Aligote, Cabernet, Fetjaska, a dry white from local grapes of that name, Negru de Purker, a red from Cabernet, Saparvi, and Rara-Njagra grapes and Romanesti from Cabernet, Merlot and Malbec grapes. From the Crimea near Yalta (of World War II fame), which has an ancient wine history, comes a rich dessert wine, Massandra Muscatel, a number of dry white and red dessert wines, and from Anapa, a Riesling. Further east, in Georgia, we find two heavy reds, Mukuzani and Saperavi, with an alcoholic content of about 14%, and two whites (about 11%) Goorjuani and Tsinandali. The area also produces champagne (or Shampanskoa). Armenia makes sweet and strong dessert wines. Russian taste tends towards sweet wines, and its wineries produce many dessert wines of between 16 & 19% alcoholic content.

Bulgaria

Many people with an interest in wines will be amazed to learn that Bulgaria, whose modern wine industry is only 34 years old, is the sixth biggest exporter of wine in the world. It is a little known statistic because the exports are mainly to the Iron Curtain countries and Germany. Bulgaria came late on the wine scene because for nearly five centuries it was ruled by the Moslem Turkish Empire. Because of its late arrival its vineyards are large and flat, and both cultivation and processing are carried on with modern machinery and scientific methods. Its best wines come from the western coast of the Black Sea, and include Riesling, Sylvaner and Chardonnay, as well as Dimiat from a local grape - a dry Riesling-flavoured greenish-yellow "white". Elesewhere we find Misket (whose derivation from Muscat is not hard to detect), a white Sylvaner type, fully fermented and therefore on the dry side: in the north a light, dry red made from the Gamza grape, the wine itself usually named after local villages; in the south a dark red named Mavrud and Pamid, a rosé drunk very young.

A Bulgarian vineyard, modern, extensive and flat. Previously a Moslem country its people did not produce wine until recently.

Assenovgrad

The traditional full red wine of Bulgaria
produced exclusively from grapes grown
in the quality wine district of Asenovgrad

1977
Mavrud

Estate BVC Bottled

Produced and bottled in Bulgaria

Assenovgrad Region

Alc 12% vol.   70cl.

Sole importer: Bulgarian Vintners Company Limited, London N1 9RD.

Hungary

There is no doubt that the first, perhaps only wine, that comes to mind from the Iron Curtain countries is Tokay. It is only one of the many Hungarian wines produced from the country's 250,000 acres, but is, without doubt, the most famous in Hungary and one of the most famous white wines in the world. It is made from three grapes, the Furmint, Harslevelu and Muskotaly, and produced in Tokay, a small village about 40 miles from the Soviet border in the north, in the Hegyalta region of the Carpathians. The grapes used suffer from "noble rot". The ripest of these are kept to allow their juice to drip without crushing, and this juice can be 60% sugar. It is known as Essencia. The normal ripe grapes are made into wine in the usual way - and called Szamorodni, the lowest quality of Tokay, and not sweet. The next highest quality, known as Aszu is made by adding the juice of the over-ripe grapes - the Essencia - to give the desired amount of sweetness. The Essencia is the highest quality of Tokay, but is so scarce as hardly to be drunk as it is. Another lesser-known wine, a red from Eger, not far from Tokay, is Egri Bikauer or Bull's Blood, dry, deep red, and slightly bitter, a wine that ages well. It is made from Kardorka, Burgundy and Medoc noir grapes. Lake Balaton, in the south-east of the country is surrounded by nearly half of its vineyards, and produces a number of wines from a variety of grapes. Best among them are: Kĕkuylü, Szukebarat, and Badascony.

Rumania

Surrounded by Russia, Hungary, Yugoslavia and Bulgaria, and with a short coastline on the Black Sea, Rumania, although it lies on the same latitude as some of the best wine-producing areas of France, has a difficult climate for wine-growing. Its winters can be bitingly cold, and its summers almost insufferable hot. Nevertheless it has over 300,000 hectares of vineyards, and produces nearly as much wine as West Germany. In fact there are vineyards in almost all parts of the country, the best of them on the eastern side. The best wines are white, made from Riesling, Aligote, Chardonnay, Pinot Gris and a variety of other grapes, including such locals as Feteasca Regal. Red wines tend to be sweet and heavy.

Yugoslavia

Yugoslavia is the tenth largest wine-producing country in the world and exports 12% of its 6,400,000 hectolitres which is a sign of the popularity of some of its wines, which have quality and are comparatively cheap. The best of them come from Slovenia in the north, from the areas of Lutomer and Maribor near the Austrian border, and include Riesling, Sylvaner, Sauvignon, Traminer and Pinot, but the vineyards of Yugoslavia extend the whole length of the Adriatic coastline to Macedonia and Serbia, east of Albania in the south, and beyond the Sav River to Vojvodina. The coastal vineyards produce both red and white wines, as do those of Serbia, while the Macedonian produce red, mainly Prokupac. Most of Yugoslavia's wines are still of the traditional types, although the areas associated with them are turning towards modern methods and grapes. Among the traditional types are a fragrant white wine made at Mostar from the Zilarka grapes, the Sipon, another sweet white wine which is said to have derived its name from French crusaders who described it as "si bon". Vojvodina, on the border of Rumania is one area where French and German wine stock are replacing the local grapes, and Kadarka, Grasevina, Ruzica etc. are giving way to the Semillons, Cabernets, Traminers etc..

Harvesting in north-west Austria, at Duernstein above (where Richard the Lion Heart was imprisoned) and at Weissenkirche.

Austria

Once one of the great wine-producing countries of the world - it embraced the old Austro-Hungarian empire - by the end of World War 1 in 1918 Austria had become one of the smallest in Europe. Today it is about eighth, producing over 8,000,000 hectolitres, most of which it consumes itself, although her export trade is growing. Most of the wine produced, certainly the best, is white, and light at that, and comes from the eastern and of the country, chiefly around Vienna the capital, Baden and Krems. Vienna, in fact, certainly deserves the wine part of "wine, women & song", for vineyards grow in the city as well as in the suburbs, and the wine they produce, known as Heurige, is drunk in the city taverns. Outstanding of the country's wine-growing regions is the Wachau, some 50 miles west of the capital, where there is a huge cooperative handling the produce of a thousand small growers. The Wachau is known for its Rhine Riesling, its Gruner Veltliner, a fresh, spicy white, green-gold in colour, and a dry wine called Schluck. Burgenland, south-east of Vienna, and on the Hungarian frontier, is known for its spátlese wines, Muller-Thurgau, Gruner Veltliner, and Muskat Ottonel, and the region contains two famous vineyards - the Esterhazy Estate and one of the vineyards of Lenz Moser, a famous Austrian viticulturist.

Cyprus

The Mediterranean island has a mixed wine history. It exported wine to Ancient Egypt, to Greece and to Rome, made wine for the crusaders, and stopped making it for 200 years while part of the Turkish Empire. Today it has a flourishing wine industry, if of very ordinary wines except for its sherry. It makes the wine with the oldest name still in use - Commandaria - a reminder of the crusades, once intensely sweet, now an ordinary commercial dessert wine. Cyprus wine was drunk at the wedding of Richard Coeur de Lion on the islands. Today only three types of grape are grown on Cyprus (on the slopes of the Troodos Mountains), as a precaution against phylloxera - Muscat, Black Mavron and white Xynisteri.

Greece

Greece has a very long wine history, and still produces much wine for its size, but few of its wines are known outside the country. The great exception, of course, is Retsina, a wine known not so much for its quality as for the fact that although it begins as an ordinary white, or occasionally rosé, wine it is given a special flavour by the addition of resin from the

A Heurige party in Burgenland.

local pine trees during fermentation. The result is not to everyone's taste by any means, but some 50% of Greek wines are treated in this way. The reason is not known - the practice goes back to the days of Classical Greece - whether the resin was added for the flavour or perhaps as a preservative is not clear.

Retsina itself comes from the region around Athens, the capital, but the largest wine-growing region is the Peloponnese area in the south, noted for its sweet wines. However, three popular white wines, Antika, St. Helena, and Demestica come from this region. The Peloponnese also produce red wines, best known of which is Mavrodaphne. In the north, in Macedonia, we find the popular red wine Naoussa. There are vineyards on most of the Cyclades, and one wine stands out, that of Samos Muscatel, a sweet dessert wine. Crete, the large Greek island south of the Cyclades, produces some strong red wines.

England

A quarter of a century ago no one would have dreamed of including England among the wine-producing countries of the world, and it must be confessed that, with only around 500 acres of vineyards, its position is humble indeed. But England in the Middle Ages made quite a lot of wine, and gave up doing so only when King Henry II married Eleanor of Aquitaine and more abundant supplies, and almost certainly of better quality became available from Bordeaux. England's northerly geographical situation means that vineyards are only likely to prosper in the southern half of the country, and the wines produced from them will be white rather than red. In recent years determined efforts have been made to revive wine production with some success within these limits. One of those who took the lead in England's wine revival is the former Marshal of the Diplomatic Corps, Sir Guy Salisbury-Jones, whose five acre vineyard in Hambledon, Hampshire produces about 12,000 bottles annually. Hambledon has another claim to fame as the birthplace of cricket. Many of England's vineyards are not much bigger, many smaller, but there are over 50 larger than 2½ acres, including such vigorous enthusiasts as Carr-Taylor's in Westfield, East Sussex and Lamberhurst vineyards in Kent. The grapes grown are chiefly Seyval Blancs and Muller-Thurgau.

Switzerland

This small country produces a great deal, and what is more, its people drink nearly all of it. Its most important vineyards are to be found on the northern shores of Lakes Geneva and Neuchatel between those bodies of water and the snubathed southern slopes of the Jura Mountains. Here, in the cantons of Vaud, Valais and Neuchatel is produced one of the country's best-known white wines, Fendant, which is crisp and dry, and named after the grape used in making it. Fendant, incidentally, is the Chasselas grape of France. The Valais also produces a good Sylvaner and Johannisberg. Although the region is noted for its white wines, some reds are also produced there, notably Dôle. In the west of the region, including the Canton of Geneva, successful experiments have been carried out with Gamay and Pinot Noir grapes for red wine. Similar developments have taken place in the south in Ticino (the Tessin) with French Merlot grapes. Some wine is produced in the region around Zurich in the north of Switzerland, but with the exception of a red wine, Klevener, made from newly introduced Pinot grapes, nothing particularly noteworthy. Switzerland has one claim to wine fame. It has the highest vineyards in Europe (3,700ft.) at Visperterminen, close to the Matterhorn.

Argentina

Few people realise it but this South American country ranks fourth or fifth among the wine-producing countries of the world. Its wines are virtually unknown outside the country itself, and the reason is obvious, for Argentina also ranks fourth in consumption per head of population, every Argentinian drinking an average of nearly 20 gallons a year - about 17 times the average in Gt. Britain. Wine production in Argentina was greatly influenced by its large Italian-origin population, immigrants of the late 19th century, and after World War II, many of whom had been viticulturists. It is, perhaps, not without significance that while Italy ranks second in the world consumption league and Spain fifth, two-thirds of the population of the country is Spanish or Italian by birth or descent. Clearly from this, most of the wine it produces is for the popular market, although some good table wines are produced, especially in the Mendoza area on the lower slopes of the Andes, where Riesling, Sauvignon Blanc and Pinot Noir grapes are grown for white wines, and Merlot and Malbec for red. For the more popular wines, Criolla or Pedro Ximenes are used for reds, and Malbec, Barbara Bonarda and Verdot for reds. In the neighbouring province of San Juan, heavy blending wines are a feature. Not only is sherry and champagne made, but, as might be expected in a country with so much Italian influence, Spumante-type wines.

Chile

On the opposite side of the Andes to Mendoza lie the principal vineyards of Chile, and it is generally recognised that they produce better wines than their Argentine equivalents, perhaps because Chile's production is only one-third of that of Argentina. There are three growing-zones - the north-west in Atacama, and Coquimbo provinces; the central region, including Santiago, from the Aconcagua to the Maule River; and a southern-central region. It is from the central region, almost facing Argentina's Mendoza across the Andes that the best wines come. They are similar to those of Bordeaux, and come chiefly from Sauvignon, Semillon, Cabernet and Merlot grapes. Although the red wines tend to be better than the white, the Rieslings from this area are noteworthy, as are also the Sauvignon Blanc and the Cabernet. The wines from the northern region, mainly from Muscat grapes, are heavy, and high in alcoholic content, much of them distilled to make a local brandy called Piseo. It is in the southern zone that we find the commoner, more popular wines, especially Pais.

Canada

Although it is grossly overshadowed by that of its neighbours, the United States, Canada does have a wine industry and, in fact, has wineries in seven of its provinces. Chief of these are Ontario and British Columbia. French colonists made wine in Canada in the 17th century, but the first commercial enterprise was in 1811, when a German immigrant started a small winery near Toronto in the province of Ontario. It was in the area south of here, on the Canadian side of the Niagara Falls that the industry first developed, and where there are now some 20,000 acres of vineyards. Grapes are also grown, and wine produced, in British Columbia in the Okanagu Valley. As in the United States the attitude towards wine is becoming more sophisticated with tastes tending towards drier wines and away from "hard liquor". In the past ten years retail wine sales increased from $100,000,000 to $400,000,000, of which 40% was imported. What are the wines produced? Name one and it will almost certainly be there. The wine list includes Sauternes and Rieslings, Clarets and Burgundies, Champagne, Tokay, Moulin Rouge, Moulin Blanc, Moulin Rosé, Sherries, Spumante, even a sparkling wine named Pussycat.

Because of Canada's weather it is necessary to raise vine-grafts under cover in the "Polyhouse" at the Bright's vineyards, whose most popular wine is President Champagne.

New Zealand

New Zealand's wine hsitory goes back some 150 years when missionaries, first English then French, took vine cuttings to the island. The commander of a ship that called there in 1840 recorded having been given a local sparkling white wine which he pronounced delicious. The wine, in fact, was made by James Busby, the Australian wine pioneer who settled in New Zealand and performed the same role there. Commercial wine production has developed and progressed since then, especially in the first thirty years or so and today New Zealand has some 2000 hectares of vineyards though the wines they produce are little known outside the country. The principal vineyards are in the neighbourhood of Auckland, notably Mount Lebanon, and further south on the east coast of North Island between Napier and Hastings, the wineries of McWilliams and Toogoods are noteworthy. There are a few vineyards on South Island but the wines they produce have little claim to fame. Much of the development of wine production in New Zealand over the years has been by European immigrant viticulturists - German, Yugoslavs and Italians among them, which probably accounts for the wide variety if not the notability of the wines produced.